Hei
Selec

Heinz Piontek

Born in Kreuzburg in 1925, Heinz Piontek has been a major presence in German literature since the 1950s. He was called up to the army while still at school, then held briefly as a prisoner of war. His lyrical poetry reflects the reactions of a generation which witnessed the collapse of the Third Reich and which matured under the new order. Piontek has translated the work of Keats, Hopkins, Yeats, Auden, Lowell and Dylan Thomas. He has also written travel prose, novels, literary criticism and radio plays. Heinz Piontek has won a number of major awards, such as the Büchner and Andreas Gryphius prizes.

Ewald Osers

Born in Prague in 1917, living in England since 1938, Ewald Osers has translated over 110 books, 31 of them volumes of poetry. His own poems have appeared in the UK, the USA and, in translation, in a number of European countries. His many translation prizes include the Schlegel-Tieck Prize, the European Poetry Translation Prize, the Austrian Translation Prize, as well as Czech, Bulgarian and Macedonian awards. Among a number of foreign honours is an honorary PhD from a Czech university and the Officer's Cross of the German Order of Merit, awarded him by President von Weizsäcker for his contribution to British-German relations.

Heinz Piontek

Selected Poems

Translated from the German by
Ewald Osers

FOREST BOOKS
London & Boston

PUBLISHED BY
FOREST BOOKS

20 Forest View, Chingford, London E4 7AY, UK
PO BOX 312, Lincoln Centre, MA 01773, USA

FIRST PUBLISHED
1994

Typeset in Great Britain by Fleetlines Typesetters, Southend-on-Sea
Printed in Great Britain by BPC Wheatons Ltd, Exeter

Original Poems © Heinz Piontek
Translations © Ewald Osers
Cover design © Ian Evans

A CIP catalogue record for this book is available from the
British Library

ISBN 1-85610-033-2
Library of Congress Catalogue Card Number 93-71942

Forest Books gratefully acknowledge the financial support for
this publication from Inter Nationes, Bonn

and the Arts Council of Great Britain

CONTENTS

FOREWORD

It is a measure of the insularity of the English reading public that a major living German poet, a man whose name is a household word in his own country and who has so much become a classic in his lifetime that he is a 'set text' in secondary school examinations, needs to be introduced to the English poetry reader.

Heinz Piontek was born in 1925, in Kreuzburg in what was then German Silesia and is now part of Western Poland. He has been a prodigiously prolific writer, not only of poetry, but also of short stories, novels, travel accounts, radio plays and literary criticism. He has edited a large number of anthologies and been the initiator and editor of a major series of some 60 volumes of poetry, short stories, novels and anthologies. He has also translated a lot of poetry: his volume of John Keats has gone into three editions, and his renderings of Dylan Thomas are outstanding for their feeling for the diction, colour and sound of the originals.

No selection from a body of many hundreds of poems can hope to be representative. While I have tried to cover different periods of Piontek's work, I make no apology for having ultimately based my selection on my own taste, on my own response to the poems.

Heinz Piontek is a 'laconic' poet: his language and imagery are compact, condensed, stripped of linguistic ballast (and indeed at times of syntactical signposts). It acts on the reader by the concision of image, phrase and allusion. Inevitably, some of the allusions – whether to German literature or to German history – will be less accessible to the English reader than to the reader of the German originals. However, with two exceptions, I have avoided explanatory footnotes; these, it seems to me, can do more harm to a poem's direct impact through the break they produce in the reader's mood than they do good by providing explication.

For most English and American readers the end of the war was a fairly well-defined moment. True, rationing and some other difficulties continued for some time, but basically there was a perceptible (and perceived) return to some kind of normality. It is important to remember that this was not the case in Germany. The shooting might have stopped, but a nightmarish situation in a country devastated materially and morally, under the (well-intentioned but sometimes insensitive) military government of the victors, with fathers and husbands often not returning from captivity for years, if at all, persisted for a considerable time.

Piontek was just old enough to be called up in the final phase of hostilities, and spent a little more than 3 months on the Eastern front. There is no mistaking the trauma of the war and its aftermath in his early poetry. An image which runs through it with great regularity is that of frost and snow – not necessarily the frost and snow of the Eastern front (which Piontek did not personally experience) as the frosty grip in which a country found itself that was short of fuel and, as a nation, traumatized by the appalling loss of life in the vast snowfields of Russia. Looking back, for Piontek, is a painful nightmare. In Casting my Mind Back he recalls the fate of the Jews:

> *. . . To the slaughter feast*
> *in the Buddenbrock settlement –*
>
> *To the small powerful Jew*
> *Ephraim –*
>
> *To the smoke.*

And in Recollection of Youth, in six short lines, he sums up his generation's experience:

> *From close to we saw*
> *black blood*
>
> *Only from afar girls,*
> *pianos.*
>
> *. . . my only support*
> *my rifle.*

The young poet struggles to discover and define his own identity:

> *Among bathers*
> *I'm not identifiable*
> *as a shipwrecked sailor . . .*

*Nothing can be read
from my lips.*

But after a while a note of defiance replaces the rearward-looking agony:

*. . . beaten, burned
as we are –*

*and no longer willing
to raise*

*brute force
once more
on our shoulders.*

It would be too facile to say that there is a swing to optimism: it is little more than a barely perceptible shift of emphasis. But is is there. In a poem entitled Learning we read that

*. . . only the word Peace
ran effortlessly
from mouth to mouth
unambiguous*

in German and English.

Yet the gap between Piontek's compatriots and the occupying forces, the wall between a still traumatized, isolated poet and the carefree German girl employee of the American Military Government – by no means a personal but a societal problem – emerges in Rendezvous: Swimming Pool.

When foreign travel becomes once more possible, the result – alongside some travel prose – are poems like Portuguese Coast and Andalusian Horses.

Unlike some of his contemporaries, who turned their backs on German literary tradition, Piontek's awareness of belonging to the mainstream is obvious – possibly more so to the German than to the foreign reader. There are echoes, deliberate or unconscious, of Goethe, Hölderin and (at least, I think so) Eichendorff, as well as references to two great medieval

German poets, Walther von der Vogelweide and Oswald von Wolkenstein. A very specific and overt reference to Goethe's *Wilhelm Meister* is in the cycle Charming Naivety or a Clutch of Classical Pages.

With advancing age we will find some social comment in Piontek's poetry – not aggressive but gently ironical. Indeed, in The Bees there is perhaps even a touch of envy for creatures untroubled by the problems of free will:

> *Totally suited to the tasks of the future,*
> *in contrast to Man,*
>
> *they identify with their functions,*
> *act unsentimentally,*
>
> *always in the social interest,*
> *knowing that Heaven is empty,*
>
> *and accepting death*
> *without questioning.*

In a more specific tongue-in-cheek poem on a meeting of the Bavarian Academy of Fine Arts – of which, of course, Piontek is a distinguished member – we read:

> *But we stand bravely*
> *by the agenda.*
>
> *Outisde, the day's agenda includes*
> *the collapse*
> *of society.*

Quite often Heinz Piontek's later poetry turns to Biblical or medieval subjects, as settings or mirrors for contemporary problems. At Night during the Building of the Tower of Babel presents an illumination from a Book of Hours:

> *A man crashes*
> *from the plank:*
>
> *just as we fly*
> *in brilliant nights*
> *shooting-star-long.*

Surely this is more than just a description of an illumination.

Throughout Piontek's poetry, from early to recent verses, a recurrent motif is that of doubt, self-doubt, doubt about the validity of words and of speech. In My Speech we find his words

> *full of doubt,*
> *not to be grasped*

and in To Achieve Something he speaks of

> *this pile of paper*
> *with its growing weight*
> *. . .*
> *But the panic*
> *about the final stretch of road,*
> *on crutches, on knees?*
>
> *The final stretch*
> *we'll be carried.*

In After Many Years he describes himself as

> *. . . still pushing*
> *the same questions before me*

and in Very Old Foolish Poet:

> *. . . waiting for his end which has*
> *long arrived.*
>
> *Not a syllable's lost over him.*

Not so. Piontek's fiftieth and sixtieth birthdays were major events in German literary life, with countless published tributes and dedicatory volumes from friends and admirers.

It is the translator's and publisher's hope that this volume, long overdue, may win him admirers also in the English-speaking world.

E. O.

Nightmares

ANKOMMEN

Windgeplagt,
mit Schneehöhlen im Gesicht.

Außentemperatur
ein Minus-Wort.

Endlich das Blut klopfen hören,
aufstampfen,

wenn Schloß und Angel
die Sicht freigeben:

auf breitgetretene Asche
toter Öfen,
das Gespenst des Feuers.

ARRIVING

Wind-tortured
with snow caves in the face.

Outside temperature
a minus word.

At last to hear the blood's beat
stamp one's foot

when lock and hinge
reveal the view:

on the trodden ash
of dead furnaces
the spectre of fire.

MADRIGAL

In our winter quarters
we drive winter out
on Rhine and Danube
in the ruined field

Though grapeshot sting like snow
Resist then, Antichrist

We drive our fires uphill

ON OLD POEMS

The expression of branches
in twelve degrees of frost –
who wrote about it?

Referred to the
incorruptible snow?

Who tried to explain what
by a tail feather
in a flurry of white?

I twist my lips
at myself.

More clearly than in the summer
I see nothing but
soot falling.

All those attempts
to fix
what no one has seen.

The radiant shape
of ice.

AUTUMN

With burning moustaches,
bald skull,
epaulettes.

Like a colonel.

Like a normally
mortal colonel.

FROM SHADOW TO SHADOW

Our days have gone with the wind.
Harsh snow lies on the garden.
How you regard me,
eye, still beautiful today.

Your unrecognized life:
where in the mist the frontier posts stood.
Not much is clarified
as far as I know.

No more about death.
But more about wordless restraint –
even though the faithful hand
be impotently clenched.

But what has been dreamed,
akin to the snow's perfume in the garden,
will move this way and that
from shadow to shadow.

CASTING MY MIND BACK

To the herb and herring barrels
of the merchant Wollny –

(I remember them clearly)

To the death-shamming dead
dragoon of Basan Heath –

To the slaughter feast
in the Buddenbrock settlement –

To the small powerful Jew
Ephraim –

To the smoke.

COME FORTH, LAZARUS

Tied hand and foot,
already shedding cheerful sweat
of the living,
yapping for air with the strength
of the gaping grave,

I – blindly,
like new wine from old skins,
God knows what for.

IN THE WATER

Among bathers
I'm not identifiable
as a shipwrecked sailor.

What's become of my future?
Above me, beneath me
nothing.

With my last ounce of strength I shape words.
Nothing can be read
from my lips.

A half-dead fish
trying to shout:
a comic sight.

NIGHT WIND

Behind us the land
we furrowed with our words.

You and I.

Nothing left but the stubble.
Swallows' droppings. In the dark the processions
with torches dipped.

Night wind, night wind:
the hollow ring of your threshing floors!

Who will get up with me,
obstinate as a mule, lower his head,
carry on?

I call outside lowered blinds,
doors without name-plates.
I look at struck sails.
I take fright.

Yes, my alarmed footsteps, this voice
of an obstinate sparrow,
not prepared to give up
what befell us
and the caked salt on the face:
Had not those who are left
better hide?

Night wind, night wind,
courier:

Is it certain
that I am the last?

Here they are, irrevocably,
your sallow eyelids
which didn't close on their own accord.
Your buried hopes, final stops,
last angry breaths.

No, the talk about you shall not cease
merely because one had had one's fill
of your corn.

Help me,
get their rifles out of the autumn,
their homeland out of the smoke,
what they promised, omitted
from our frontiers

and add it all to the years
by which one must stand -

as the dandelion by the hay
the stoneware by the fire,
dead or alive.

But what next?

Does the spared pine-tree
reveal its intentions
before the next felling?

Up there in the darkness
where the highest branches are lost
in the uncontrolled rustle far above ground

it rallies all its needles
so it should not cease -
this dry half-audible ringing.

Night wind, night wind:

What more can we try to do
than be loyal -

whatever that means

RECOLLECTION OF YOUTH

Never seen
hops,
let alone
a vineyard.

And yet stretched out
under other light
leaves:

my uncouth youth.

It seems
we spoke a
hard language.

From close to we saw
black blood.

Only from afar girls,
pianos.

Suddenly I,
the youngest
among us shadow-throwers,

had that unsteady gait –

my only support
my rifle.

FALLING ASLEEP

At night there was nothing
to be heard.

No crazy clatter
of gas-masks and beakers.
No neighing of horses.
No shell-bursts.

We lay back
and dropped
into darkness

as into a shoe
called childhood.

CALL-UP CLASSES

With cudgel
music

With the frozen meat
medal

With nothing

but a green
twig

> For Günter Eich
> on his 60th birthday

NO LONGER WILLING

Is it true
we're getting ossified?

Has peace now lasted
too long?

Our shaky peace
bought with loss of blood,
tear salt and mutilations.

That's right: settle accounts
with us
cowards:

beaten, burned
as we are –

and no longer willing
to raise

brute force
once more
on our shoulders.

ON SUCH A NIGHT

The bells swathed
sore from smoke
we escaped
to our tavern.

Bright crows in the brushwood:
lumps of snow.
The dark eaves of the roof
sagging.

With scorched eye-lashes
the young lady slipped out of her furs
and threw herself round my neck –

on such a night
between two peasant wars
in the heart of Brabant.

LET'S BE CLEAR

Autumn is
a wildfire.

What will
winter be:

Our dispersal
is under way.

Who or what
will survive the winter?

Don't try
to fool me!

SAFE CONDUCT

A bank will
remain.
Or the end of a
field path.

Beyond the last lights
our road will lead us.

We must not be stopped
by anyone or anything!

Our mouths
will then be
full of laughter –

Our souls
ready for the journey –

The universe
but a narrow
door,

flung open wide –

POSTSCRIPT

Now we must believe in it:
Everything is renewed through water,
the word in the water.

The message and
the language which I
find again in shining lumps.

Man, unrecognizable,
without cloak or excuses answers for his guilt
of his own will.

On this side the fight continues with the wolves
in the thorax.
On the other: no promise.

High up and very bright in the tree-tops
I spot an increasingly
green certainty,

you men and brothers.

Recovery

OLD STUDENTS

Cloaks in the wind
and from Prague,
making music –

who will once more
forge a romance
to make us prominent?

November and
sheets of music blown
into our faces.

Behind the windows
the officials are
laughing.

Thus we shuffle
from one foot
to the other –

but the last ship
has sailed

and from the castles
the farewell is sounded.

JOURNEY'S END

Earth on which I'm flying
at vintage time.

At night the small coins for my acting
clattering on scrubbed tables.
Armistice.

The Residence
is haunted by the chill.

Many now, laughing, travel
to New Orleans,
to the autumn fair.

But what does "Follow your nose" mean?
I ask this volte-
face age.

Quicklime awaits me.
Not the pale shade
of the Lusam Grove.*

First a wall for dogs
and bullets.

* in the centre of Würzburg, according to tradition the burial place
of Walther von der Vogelweide, the mediaeval German poet.

WRITING

Imagined lines:
air corridors.

Words as a beacon
in the outer ear.

Possibilities
of reaching a port.

One's life is
at stake.

WIND-SWEPT LEAF

Deceived
Deceived

You are not
you

At the time
of stars being sung to nothingness

Deceived

At the time
when the murderers rest

Deceived

At night
in the creeping to groaning ships

Or else

you were not
you

TO HEISENBERG'S DISCIPLES

Greek
my work may
be to you.

With the goose-quill.

The results of your
incomprehensible apparatuses
seem to me

Outdatable.

Ignorant
we turn a cold shoulder
on each other.

Separately
we approach
common ground.

PEACE SONG

Untroubled we lie together,
the air is clean.

Peace isn't making much
ado.

In the forest the huntsmen
shoot rose-red.

It pleases us to take the sleighs
through deep snow,

sail on the Danube
by the light of matches.

In Backnang or Munich
the air is once more clean.

The sky is worthy
of watching.

FIFTHS ON THE HORN

Up, finch and siskin,
up, thrush,
into the Occident!

A morning like sugar floss.

Everything fast
turns orange.

Two who once more
intertwine
their fingers –

What is it, maple and elm,
that disturbs you?

What's the matter with the grass?

You on the battlement,
speak up!

LEARNING

Alongside their ox carts
natives strangely
spoke to us.

We tried to guess.

The oldest amongst us worriedly
talked of seven hundred kilometres
separating them from their
young wives.

We tried to understand.

The first newspapers
as if printed
white on black.

we began to spell.

Only the word Peace
ran effortlessly
from mouth to mouth,
unambiguous,

in German and English.

HOW MUSIC STRUGGLED THROUGH

At midday a girl came
into the dining hall
of the community kitchen
(poor-house kitchen).

From the front in the north she
had wandered to that in the south,
with nothing
but a dusty violin case.

Gladly she took a few spoonfuls
of groat soup,
the case on her knees.

Everyone saw the cohesion
of her straight shoulders.

Before disappearing
she bowed for us
all four strings;

small scars in her face
were turning bright red.

Appreciatively we rapped
our knuckles
on the table –
Unsuspecting we hailed

the survival of
a classical theme.

UTOPIAN POEMS

1.
Civil war, in the end
you'll be the last
civilian left.

2.
Street battles between colours,
birthdays, genitals,
the pages of one and the same book.
No quarters given.

3.
Cities, you'll once more
be transparent.
The dream of the uncomplicated passes
through fire.

4.
In barricaded houses
money once more
assumes Renaissance shape.

5.
Rope and pit
for privileged cases.
We'll be left lying
on the pavement.

6.
Ah yes, peace:
to be experienced only through force.

7.
Glorious life
of bandits,
leaving their problems
to their captain's beard bristles
while camping on the roofs with wenches.

8.
Once more the unread
will be the more knowledgeable.

9.
In the country
all will tremble.

10.
Defeatist!

UNDER THE ALPS

1.
Bad weather like wisps of hay
hanging from the trees.

And the slogans: That Yes doesn't mean Yes,
that a rope's ready for me –

But in actual fact: What I omitted,
wrote into the chimney stack –

vanity
our garrotte –

Nothing more comes to my ear
over the mountains.

2.
An apple, green-peeled.
With it Tyrolean wine.

The rain is stopping.
Yesterday I was in despair.

Already the air is clearing.
My courage is growing.

In advance
I demolish the words

with which I might sail
over the mountains.

SPELLING OUT

With a voice
that falters –

With a calculation
gone wrong –

The only honesty
from a few

courageous
vowels.

OSWALD'S STONE STATUE, BRIXEN

Chubby-cheeked gentleman, mid-twenty.
Beard and spurs
foppish.

The fearless
songs from these lips,
to earn a living.

I want something to remain
as it is.

Really not to be removed:
war, shady deals, the heavy
sail of his thoughts –

of one cast.
Yet love through
five-hundred years

more delicate than hand-weighed
apricots.

(Note: Oswald von Wolkenstein, 1377–1445, a native of
the South Tyrol, one of the major German Minnesänger,
the courtly lyrical poets.)

BUTTER MARKET IN KREUZBURG

How beautiful you are, sun,
shining by the pound from baskets
full of damp leaves.

Wrapped in skirts, petticoats
and dust-sheets
they're selling you
they're being sold.

They're rarely washed
as well as you are.
But the tongues,
their lonely tongues.

(Laughing
speaking a difficult language.)

PORTUGUESE COAST

The old sea routes are inked lines
made with green wine.
When the wind goes ashore
it rains cards and tricorns.
Now the melancholy discoverers ride
into the oats.
Now peacocks, white as salt, come
form the convents.
The sea remembers
only dimly.

ANDALUSIA'S HORSES

Frivolously
tiptoeing on their hooves:

the real and secret
adversaries
in the bull's shadow.

Their tails have the grace
of sanguine temperaments.

They paw the ground for the
just-vanished sun.

Behind their fly-string
they're like a perfume like the mountains
where the snow is burnt.

PRECURSORS

We were stragglers.
The weather has changed.

The message was universally known.
Now it is a rumour,
credible only to cash registers in shopwindows.

Precursors who crossed themselves
have vanished in the bushes on both sides
the lot of them.

Ahead is nothing but a very wintry light.
Now we are the spearhead.

But whose precursors could we be
when behind us the field is empty
except for the hares' snow-white bones?

No stormy petrels!

Instead we must
learn the trade of the first swallows.

SONG ON A HAY BARGE

Still on this side, my life,
clocks in the east,
night still
at my shoulder:

Two birds with
pale red beaks fighting
through the grey
of your blouse.

We're drifting, neglected,
salt on our eye-lashes,
barred the harbour,
we two without lanterns,

like mutineers at the end:

you sea-shell,
I lead-weight.

STRANGE

Stand. Go.

Still at night
with the confidence
of the morning

on the knife's tip.

And platonic
love, the clouds.

Joyous beacons

where through the bushes
rings out the night's Who-goes-there.

CRYSTAL CLEAR

The metaphor
is a telescope.

It arms
the eye.

Focuses.
Magnifies.
Sharpens.

Clear and close
we see
the truth.

Seemingly.

BILLETDOUX

Come
for bell and cockerel
already rehearse something classical
for three voices

Come
for between the flagstones
the hungergrass is growing
fat

Come
yes come and wring
the bright water
from sail canvas

Come
with a cap
full of wind
to our bolt-straight jetty

Come
and put
my burning impatience
in the shade

TREES

You yes you.

With calm foothold
on the dark earth.

But vulnerable
like us

who must fight their
way forward.

Useful or
simply beautiful

and invariably
meaning something new.

To grow thus:

to the heights,
to the depths,

and with
arms flung open.

For Alfred Focke

LITANY FOR VON DER VRING

Behind the watercolours of rain-washed gardens
behind patrician houses school clocks canals
behind the hay and straw of flowers
behind summer and autumn

behind the word Flanders
behind the lips of a Swabian woman
behind blue haze like the legend of white
floating hair and the corpse
dragged ashore

behind obstinacy folly love
behind the fully paid price
behind a dyke on the Weser

you'll be roused from the dead by
the silver-throated horns of your poems

NOT WITH WORDS

How shall I prove it to you,
the Emperor's friend?

Snow-white is the future.
An unwritten page.

I think of letters which are older
than metal.

And now of something that
is independent:
absolute.

That's what I believe in.
You'll see.

For if I survive
in the snow-drifts of my winter quarters –
as a proof?

Your hands are still in
your pockets.

Observe me closely!

I, ANTON PAVLOVICH

am shamming health,
polishing my pince-nez,
observing the incurable.

The only member of my guild
I have seen the whites in the eyes of deportees,
recorded screams, cudgel blows,
the source of lunar heat
on the ice-sheet of Sakhalin.

God has fortified my memory,
for do I not write again
of bored young girls,
pampered scoundrels, green and
grey blockheads

and have the nerve
to write even
of a field full of cherry-trees?

These lists of names, references
to landed estates which I
send to the theatres.

The truth
must be kept out of sight,
I make long pauses
between words.

Thus I earn some sweated money
with plays that are flops.

If the old applaud me
it is for lack of something better;
the young sneer at my white
gloves, they want
to see blood.

I hear them already
around the
freshly dug pit:

Oh, if only he hadn't
been so indecisive!

As if I had not
from the very start
protested against the lie.

(Note: "Have I not all my life protested against the
lie?" – Anton Chekhov)

STAY INDOORS

What is it you want, wind,
with the creaking of frames?

Your free will:
no contentious issue
for casuists.

Something that I
consolidate through myself –

perhaps
my errors.

And outside,
the one-way streets
full of revolutionaries:

no one
following himself.

The direction justifies
the conscience.

Wisdom

DAVID

1.
Days and nights cowering, doubled up,
you on your roof,
higher than Zion's many balconies.

Eyes, veiled by congested blood:
too weak
to discern the fig orchard to one side
and the flags of the sand-storm
on the other.

And the inward frost,
the shivering from the spine.
Yet you are covered with furs in abundance,
with carpets from the tents.

2.

Darkness falls. Calmly as ever
the fifteen-year-old approaches.
Abisag from Sunem.

Today with your old man's claw
you strike her, who night-long
slept in your arms, a source of warmth,
softly out.

Already she is no more.

But the thorny thicket
in your rib-cage?

Tatters of thoughts.

Cause of all causes:
Why did.
The first-created.
Allow primal evil.
To penetrate into them
as through a leak –

Rebellion?

And does this tormenting restless
grinding in the heart remain
to the end?

3.

Not one,
ten lives you've lived.
Yes, you.

Under the
shadow of His wings.

Anointed.
Victorious. A golden jewel
among the psalmists.

Aeons later –
as the host of stars
in a desert night:
your descendants.

And do you surmise
that His greatest promise of love

– reconciliation with all
and for always –

through one mortally despised,
a man of pain,
will first reach *Your people*?

You're brooding still over the incidents
of your apostasy.
All,
all of them He made you pay for.

Misfortunes.
Cudgel blows.

4.

Now,
as though you were lying in a shaking mill,
the roof-tiles are trembling:
from the penultimate, ultimate
terrible jerk of your heart.

Below you in the chambers,
among servants, slave girls and dogs
nothing is felt.

Only Bath-Sheba is holding her breath, listening;
moist salt in the furrows
of her face.

The millstone has stopped.

5.

Just then from the flat roof
invisible eddies rise
of whirring, roaring, rushing:

like nothing on earth –

not even those rarely perceived
flying sounds
of desert herons migrating in squadrons –

not even in a dream.

CHARMING NAIVETY
or A CLUTCH OF CLASSICAL PAGES

1.
How mild the summer is.
From the chimney-pots
on the tavern roofs in the market
pale flags are flying.

Here W.
encounters the wreckage
of a recently failed
actors' company:

She, under a black mantilla,
in a white, not quite clean but
comfortable negligé, swaying lightly
on her delicate
high-heeled slippers –

He, his rapier under his arm,
fonder of lunging that walking,
presently from a blue bag pours
roasted almonds into her lap –

Both are still very young,
W. is but a few years older.

2.
On joint excursions to the country
they come, on one occasion, to a former mill,
where they pleasurably feast
and in naive tone
chat uninhibited,
sharp as needles.

All round them is nothing
but splendid old trees
and grass in their shade.

3.
In the long luminous evenings
they lie in the windows
of their tavern,

amusedly watching the antics
of a troop of tumblers, rope-dancers,
snake-men and a muscle-man,
cheered by half the township.

Among the acrobats
a girl of thirteen
with a rather boyish body
and dusky skin.

W., after one single
glance, cannot
take his eyes off her.

4.
But now the fragrance and gleam
of half a novel must first float past

before W. gets as close
to the secret of Mignon
as is possible.

LAST VOYAGE

Although it is on its way
to the wrecking and scrapping berth
at the edge of the shipyard,

I still admire
this windjammer,
as, sides and superstructure
all of white or brownish gold,
it floats, sails reefed,
over the harbour basin –

while a small
sooty tugboat,
only its smoke-flag gold-threaded,
tows it along.

Misty blue above the ships' hulls
below them reflections in the water
like barrels full of coins.

Your colours,
William Turner.

THE ROOFTREE

When I shaded my eyes
I saw
the nostalgic end of the roof:

the final verse,
rhythmically chanted by hollow bricks.

I thought of the aura
of chimneys:
crude carbon, birdlime,
shadow of cats –

and our
free fall.

Long shirts of lovers
were hanging from a dormer window.

But I saw the radiant morning
on the rooftree's shoulder.

Felt it tremble
as if under caresses
at aircraft noises and the sounds
from towers.

And I dreamed
I was walking that ridge:
careful, farsighted,
closest to clarity.

SLIVOVITZ

Uphill
in the shade of plum-trees:
Let me embrace you all!

Water falls vertically
into troughs.

Still no one has
a key
to the barns in the rock.

The double-bass, the comb,
the embroidered shirt.

Silently I drop
on a
sheaf of Serbian straw.

RENDEZVOUS: SWIMMING POOL

There we lay in the afternoon
around a shabby swimming pool.

Over there was the forest,
were the mountains.

And here the junior doctors,
discharged paymasters, brunette
girl students and a blonde
from the military government:

lively and a pleasant sight
in her swimsuit –

amidst a more silent majority
entirely among themselves.

Oh to be part of a group!
Thus I though,
edging closer,

longing
to share her relaxed laughter,
never to be short of an answer!
But the air, the forest, the frontier barracks
and a swallow bisecting the light
bewitched my tongue.

So I buried my freshly bathed
head in my arms.
So the decision fell.

TERRA INCOGNITA: POEMS

Here
still a blank patch
and I, the native.

Here
are printed letters
my footprints.

Behind
deleted words
I lurk.

Retrieve
me with your gaze
into the inhabited world.

CIRCA 1800

Graceful the curtsey
of the subject children

while some princely foot
is stamped.

Lines of poetry.
Cudgel blows.

Many dream
of being sold.

The ink shines bright.

Germany's
classical age.

COPPER ENGRAVING

Old piles of stones
in prints,

called cities.

My oldest experiences
which
I never had:

The counting of the sand grains
on my death sentence
till it dries;

the muffled drum roll;

a sudden flash of Jerusalem,
not distant now.

LEAVING THE CITY

In the main streets the young
unconcernedly compete
in their splendour.

The old are lurking
behind suburban windows.

We have here
no abiding city.

It is true, I omitted
to talk to you brokenly
of one to come.

Kinds of death excited us,
not the kinds of
resurrection.

And yet, at times it was
my tongue

that, having tasted
wine, fruit, other lips,
salt and blood,
oppressed me:

Is that all?

Unbelieving
I sought and sought –
even behind the words,
the best of all words.

Now I leave them behind.

Unconditionally
I turn to a future
unencumbered by yesterday.

THE BEES

Creatures figuring in proverbs.
Examples of division of labour.

Top to toe in a weatherproof fur,
beneath it armour.

Their tools are precise
and efficient.

Two hundred wing-beats
per second.

Formerly forest creatures,
now, untamed, living alongside us.

They show no mercy
to drones, invaders, effete intellectuals.

*Every state must have its standing army
of bees.* (Sprengel)

Totally suited to the tasks of the future,
in contrast to Man,

they identify with their functions,
act unsentimentally,

always in the social interest,
knowing that Heaven is empty

and accepting death
without questioning.

ACADEMY OF FINE ARTS

Not over the rooftops –
carried up by lifts we arrive

Our wigs are unpowdered.

"My writer friend,
that is: he was jealous of me.
and I deeply mistrusted him
while we greatly esteemed one another."

After black coffee we start
our vigorous tight-rope dance
on ropes on the floor.

"Yes, I once rubbed shoulders with Rilke."

Then we wrap up,
working on our pipes,
while the smoke wafts across
to the Bohemian horizon.

The dialogues cool
as the wind long ago in the colonnades
of the plane trees.

"I quote: All beauty
must die one day."

But we stand bravely
by the agenda.

Outside the day's agenda includes
the collapse
of society.

ABOUT A ONCE-BURNT PERSON AND HIS PERVERSE FIRE

For Reiner Kunze

Where even a wisp of smoke
from the ashes
seems treason,

where the words *Danger Zone*
are bitten back, where hands are cupped
over a struck match,

on hills outlined green
and closely scanned:

he feeds with his verses
a small wide-awake
light-giving fire –

as if under our
humanist sun we were
groping in darkness.

TO ACHIEVE SOMETHING

This century and
my attempts

to achieve something.

This pile of paper
with its growing weight.

Under my jacket I hid
the brash coronary.

At times I was propped up
by monosyllables.

But the panic
about the final stretch of road

on crutches, on knees?

The final stretch
we'll be carried.

READING TOUR

Maybe
the bank of the Main,

a warm gust of air
under the Dolomites –

The evening
is reached only
by the outside staircase:

and what is established,
the pages gone brittle,
you turn them:

touchstones,
milestones –

you turn them.

MY SPEECH

> . . . the truth and nothing
> but the truth

Snow-white gently-level land,
where the colour of farm-carts
set on sled-runners
tried to cling,

where at night the white half-shadow
of hair loosened in sleep
over neck and shoulders
would wander –

If in white words all this
shows through the paper
like a watermark:

unrestricted,
full of freedom to doubt,
not to be grasped –

How then can my speech be:
Yea, yea – ?
Nay, nay – ?

AFTER MANY YEARS

The mass of water
at Ulm:

Renewed encounter with something
hard to see through,

something that's always rolled on
to who knows where,

ultimately
not to be deflected –

and I: still pushing
the same questions before me,

with human perseverance,
obviously,

still restless and still
a little hasty –

even the bed
that recalls my own:

certain places
where our dissolution begins.

AT NIGHT DURING THE BUILDING OF THE TOWER OF BABEL

(IN A BOOK OF HOURS)

Below, in the fire's glow
lime and hewn stone.

By the block and tackle
the slogan makers.

But who would trust the smile
of the bucket-bearers

from step to step?

Above, where now
the stargazers lean,

from the uppermost gallery,

a man crashes
from the plank:

just as we fly
in brilliant nights,

shooting-star-long.

OLD MASTERS

1.

They lived among peasants, messengers,
abbots and huntsmen.

2.

Of their teachers
I still see
the mountains
and the Lech
with mule-grey billows.

3.

Above, in the vault scaffolding,
before perspectives
with tortured
saints, nuns, church benefactors,
winged children,

they received pale blue
and pink
in winched-up buckets.

4.

All this I accommodate
in my writing.

5.

But what would their thoughts have been
about the ground of their paintings,
their time, losing itself
in green fields?

6.

What mattered or counted
for an established painter
as he lay awake upstairs in his
low-ceilinged room,

downstairs a new-born child
or a dead wife?

7.

And did they, in the morning,
with pulled-in bellies fall upon
their knees,

while the luminous dry
spirit of the eighteenth century
held sway,

asking for favour –
before once more taking up dividers,
pocketing chalks and
a pouch of tobacco?

8.

No thoughts handed down to us,
only bills of account.

VERY OLD FOOLISH POET

Alone with himself
among bitten pipe-stems and a sackful
of manuscripts.

Even his last pure joy,
the books –
he can scarcely decipher them,

can no longer run into all the taverns
with his damned heart.

Meanwhile the teeth-gnashers are writing large
their names over small poems,
poetesses prance perilously
on his home ground.

Thus he sits, a pair of patient buttocks,
his nose, offended, in the air,
waiting for his end which has long
arrived.

Not a syllable's lost over him.

But when all is lost,
cherry-red like Poland
the day will come –

but for whom!

Other German Titles Published by
FOREST BOOKS

Pied Poets
Translated and edited by Robert Elsie

An anthology of contemporary Romanian Transylvanian and Danube poets writing in German
Dual text English/German
A somewhat frivolous poetic tombstone which marks the passing of the 'fifth German literature', that of the German minority of Romania.

ISBN 0-948259-77-9   paper £8.95   208pp

Step Human into This World
Poems by Olav Münzberg
Translated by Mitch Cohen and Ingrid Stoll
with a foreward by Hans Christoph Buch

Travel poems from the fall of the Berlin Wall to Tianamen Square. Poems which express great feelings towards the survivors of the Holocaust and other victims of German history, yet also express an internationalism and solidarity with the poor and the oppressed of the Third World.

ISBN 0-948259-53-1   paper £8.95   144pp

An Anthology of Sorbian Poetry from the 16–20th Centuries
Translated and edited by Robert Elsie
Illustrated by Sulke Ulbricht

The Sorbs are a Slavic race in what was East Germany. This collection is the first to be made in an English translation.

ISBN 0-948259-72-8   paper £6.95   96pp

Young Poets of Germany
Translated by Raymond Hargreaves
Edited by Uwe-Michael Gutzschhahn

This anthology introduces the work of 27 poets all born between 1952 and 1962 and brought up in one or other of the two German states. Wry, laconic, full of a sense of loss or deprivation. These diffuse and dissenting voices are all characterised by a sense of displacement and dislocation.

ISBN 1-85610-032-4   paper £8.95   160pp